fluttertongue

Book 1: The Book of Games

fluttertongue

Book 1: The Book of Games

Steven Ross Smith

Canadian Cataloguing in Publication Data

Smith, Steven, 1945 –

Fluttertongue

Poems.
ISBN 1-895449-79-0

1. Title.

PS8587.M59 F58 1998   C811'.54   C98-920175-9
PR9199.3.S5616 F58 1998

Book and cover design by J. Forrie
Art Direction A.M. Forrie
Typeset by Thistledown Press Ltd.
Cover painting: *Good Times* by Anne McElroy

Printed and bound in Canada by
Veilleux Impression à Demande
Boucherville, Quebec

Thistledown Press Ltd.
633 Main Street
Saskatoon, Saskatchewan
S7H 0J8

THE CANADA COUNCIL | LE CONSEIL DES ARTS
FOR THE ARTS | DU CANADA
SINCE 1957 | DEPUIS 1957

Thistledown Press gratefully acknowledges the financial assistance of the Canada Council for the Arts, the Saskatchewan Arts Board, and the Government of Canada through the Book Publishing Industry Development Program for its publishing program.

contents

v. a game to be played

for bp

*Madness is language is how you use it   if you are not mad you use it
one way   if you are mad you use it another way   these are not
categories   there are many ways of both ways*

— bp Nichol

i. white cycle (extracts)

5.

"Experience grows
naiveté the teacher"

"There is space here
where peers evaluate"

(essence of nothing
rien in another tongue)

"Exponential is a kind of growth"

groping for expansion
a symbol may be
reinterpreted

"Resistance offers no answer
to this question of doing"

& doing is
written down

a resumé is not
existence   is no evidence
breathing will not signify

"Why not"

it is no season for beginning
i can tell you, i've
just begun, become
a moment   lifting

my diaphragm draws
(parted from this breathing
i am no more than

m o l e c u l a r v i b r a t i o n

energy is transferred
to phosphorescent screens

streams through space
escapes
to exhibition

7.

golden &
harder than others
yet more malleable
   gilt
   gift

   a gregarious stream
   tarnished with insensitivity

i am talking here of language
   using language
      licking the quill's tip

   integrate totality
   with segments
       segue
         out of function
  into glitter
  all that   is not gold

older ogres are no more frightening
     (the consonant
     silent & useless)
       than our evocation
     (out of place)

"My grand consideration
is no more than this goal"

all elemental or
ganic
available to kings
)& crazies(

       bold gesture
       out of madness
       turns vocal
       sometimes to willing softness
       contains a tongue
       & teeth a
       grit
       grinding

8.

husband
reference not wanted
rules are fixed without referees
this spouse starts off
couple halved (one of two used)
in one context
content
& yet denying

      the consonant is sometimes silent
          not constantly
     of flesh
     or of the spirit
     the reference is to *tangible*
         & handled

he may stray
in mind
is held
(bind is tight)

       resistance bound
      to stunt this writing
       disband the act
        of hand
       moving
        slight &
        magically
       quicker than the

                    i see the movement
                     h o l l o w
                    as some are

heads of households
hustle &
bust an artery
                    description
                    almost harangue
                                    a lemon (a herring)
                                      in the midst

                    definitely muscle
                      & hungry

                              17

11.

kept
castled
the dark administration

> sits in my dream
> stark
> it is oppression
> life shrouded
> the inkling of a trap

mary's hand is on the door   it clicks   is open

no hope for black characters
movement is vague, beneath
sudden shadows
letters shift

> unsensed
> shallow
> held back
> do not flow
> are sometimes silent

>> forgotten
> know no firm position

>> a person
>> comes and goes
>> in front of eyes
>> cowers, in
>> worthlessness
>> reveals a lack

            cancel life
      you have no living
                  quick
impulse is measured
      by momentum
                              kilometres
                        the   metric
                  measure of this   breath's line

killing stops
breathing and the word
                              energy is tension
                              still crackles

12.

lips
slip   spill
over a cheek
into a mouth   tongues slick through
                                porcelain
                                cracks wide
                                the passage is entered
                hand slides
                moves to curves
                comes to purple
                violets
                        (no violence)
                tips firm   pulsing
        in the loose fittings there is room to breathe

the minstrel haunts the night
his song
beneath the moon
intones a pale mood

luna
your skin is opaque
shadows move
across enamel   blinks
erase reflection

                        quick!
                        this earth sinks behind eclipse
                        viewed in binoculars

turns larger
with dimming dimension

>the illustration
>is no loss
>a lift against gravity
>a gain made
>limits moved outward

>a kiss
>complete
>luminescent

14.

                    night
                    a new alluring
                    but
                                black
                    a raven's back

                    darkness settles
                    chemical death
                    sprayed fine
                    on plant's leaves
                    nothing
                    will replace
                    their colours
                                        brown
                                        into the earth
                                        this wilting carries them
wet murder on my hands
caring comes too late
finger tip caress is
futile
                breath
is final
                    night
                    sends secret messages
                    i am not touching you

                    my hands are clean
                    washed of the smell of soil

blooms
        blemishes
there is a garden living
     a garden dead
the sun is gone
permits a hiding

my stomach turns
weighs
denial
       apology
in regret i go numb

15.

organization is not arbitrary
but striven for
the group's symmetry laid out
this is music

organist touches keys
wind becomes melody, the tones
mournful
tunes
        spices lie in
                a kiss
   placed
           on your mouth
"gone are the days" they say
"turning thirty"   & i am
(a half or a third is reached)

men embrace publicly
chests press together
love is open

the low dirty moon
shines everywhere
moans over my birth
my mother labouring
she is pretty
young and screaming with me

i come properly
changing universes, one
of liquid to one
of flesh
(the only time)
screeching my complaint

a keen edge cuts between

        imprint begins

                 :discord
                 :dissonance

tear me again
mother, touch me
fill with tears
the years since
the scissored separation

16.

1. professional night games seem to indicate
   money
           (purpose is avoided)

2. paleontological evidence indicates
   they have always existed

               perhaps there is a throw
               that excels
               or maybe the thrower

               promises are broken by
               performance
               (or lack of it)

broken lives
bloody images
high pay
high price

                           in chairs
                           the quiet spirits die

           "definitely this is
           not appeasement"

place a hand on flesh to heal

           "the last indication is
           of more"

monotony betrays its own plan
the game proceeds
without surcease
the crowd is tuned
tips on cue

                         (release us from the trap)
                                   no!
                            we dare not
                            find the catch
                           afraid to field
                              the dark

17.

quite like dragon teeth
this clenching
   clean white enamel
    is not under the jaw
words are held to equation

       breast
       a mother offers
       dries

       shivers to the quick
                & eloquent pronouncement
                adjectives deleted
                the noun is strong
                (description made quiet)
                     is itself
       arc in air
       pierced bulls-eye
       flight stopped
       the arrow quivers
       narrows where the bound
       is stricture

the answer rests
the question is conditioned
loss sounds as
a scream

delinquents draw up
communiqués & dogma, distribute energy
                    there is promise
                    the soldier equipped
                    (equated with statistic)

substitutes are offered
the candy
            dry & crumbling
                                        equinox upon us
                        he coughs
                        his spittle
                        is his blood
                                        the trumpets blare
                                        unequal

18.

rigorous
this method of extraction

simplicity is moved to
the injury
          (remedies itself)
slice the melody in sections
reveal its secrets, certainly
the track is found
though no recollection is distinguished

                              there is a cast
                              flows to resolution
                              strikes a final die

                              somewhere in the desert
                              a bell chimes
                              haunting colours born
                              out of elements
                              (the camels do not move)

                              convey this destiny
                              to its carriers
convex arc in flight plan
                    & still the desert sand
                              teeth are not images
                              the tongue bitten
                              incites a moan
                              lips lunge for the throat

a kiss
a fatal calculation
there are no reasons
the real thrust is felt
inside the stomach
the kick sharp & painful

beneath
locked lips
the cleft is
soft
moist
the cry is deep & from the loins

lions walk uneasy in this night   all is as suspended   awaits reproach

19.

sonnets were created are
created measures
a way of indicating
        time & so
        the net is cast
        while early sun
        cracks on the cold atlantic
        before moving high
        overhead
                "o for heat"
                a cry
                a voice almost human
                benign

ten stem from one root
this first is tense
risk is minimized
the format is contained

                "you remind me of . . ."
                (your breasts at least)
                me a suckling
                "promise me no teasing"

investigation is the key
there are other voices
        other serpents tonguing

            a kiss in air
            divided

repentance is no longer
necessary

as with repetition
    repetition

         small
         you are my
         china doll

o
i feel the rhythm
the lines are tight
the closing is in sight

20. *for henri chopin*

throats
some open them
press
        the lines are marked in wood
            e   (ascending)
        e
    e   tubular
    e
e   & dimensional
e
the laser pulsates   ooooooooooo (a low moan)
                    a horn in the tunnel
                    voices come through
                    sounds we are not accustomed
to tense
        the separation is distinct where
        thunder echoes
                                    & in the peanut butter
                                    is a crunch
        under the tongue
        vibration waits
                    mmmmmmmmmmmmm (the deepest) a tuba

        you promise me an open landscape
        my voice no longer just a word

(hearing this you are past a resonation)

                    sona

                        soma

                            sola

                                solo

                                  sole

                                    so late

         my soulstice sun   adrift

i hear them come   (there are no reasons to deny)

                                  indication

                                  : lips in space

        she cries

        "you are heat & tension

        be tender in my branches plurality"

      fleura   light   sea

           defies translation

21.

universal, scope
is to be expected
is a stumbling
block

    ale passing
    down my throat
        a bubble
    that history
    moves inside
    bursts an entry
    to the atom's centre

    minuteness is economy they say

you are not mute
inherently
this is space
(outer)
out of reaches of the mind
& inside
definition is insisted
    is delineated
a linearity to move from
      (cock hardens)
rigidity
to make yourself small in
    one verse
    the whole poem
    for utility
    is there room here for utopia

judged myopic
he accepted distortion
reality too painful
(unless there is a vision
there is no hope)

                    the clock rests
                    a quarter past the moon
                    change is made in silver
                    doubled
                              for a follower
fall low &
do not rise again
              or   stand & howl
                    the secret is cosmic breathing
                    uttered impromptu

22.

vanished stars link
& family ties
father & son

(book still unread
this thinking is a record)

                    mill wheels turn
                    create rhythm
              & production, raw
         materials are provided

vision divided
eye from eye
threading slow velocity

              a varnish coat covers
                  finishes clear
                is visible at edges

there is virtue
in the act itself
select and true
the image is
inscribed

          visit me, i will
          tell you of long nights
          new vectors to
          fracture a song

promise me simplicity
names
like buenos aires & kiev

i will change identity, disappear
in roles, relate through different selves, cells
to search

the corners are removed
effort in full view

23.

with (little effort)
a preposition moves through
the sentence into childhood
close to heroes
information is withheld
diagnosis incomplete

welcome the double letter sounded once
a bell chimes in it

across the lake
waves shuffle
a light is blink-
         ing

certainly the score is even

"wire the whole world"
"with smiling"

"save energy
for consequence"

you
both of you
you double
you dance
a duplicate

wishing rises from below
promise is broken
a willow arches

transcendent
there is no weep
though a leaf is out of hand

        suddenly the acts are sane
        wisdom saving us

wake up with electricity
turn off the clock radio

        this vibration
        invigorates a wave length
        a mirror
        a wow

ii. a stranger's dream

WE RUN

we run across dunes
naked   legs   churn
sheening heat bars ripple horizons
storms liquefy the nerves
desire's spiral arms strain for contact

(lacking we discover the deception
shelter. virtual ceilings collapse on
scrutiny. {see: horizontal degeneration})

in formation overhead information satellites
whisper   magnify to tenth power
in the granular sea relay stations rise
raised on machines
eloquent in binary tongues

skin in motion lags weakened
in the silicate hurricane
flesh evaporates
a thin mirage
seen in cindering eyes

CRACKS

we hide inside thin names, some
times hold the body steady. i
taste and walk with articulate
concern

a blade

your shining self   in
stream or leaf   or sky
guides me through screens   the
                                        crack
                                                    of bliss

i turn
away. you shatter circuits. ignite
internal movies. pierce near my heart. i watch the
flame's narcotic
burn. deny.
watch the orange orchids
yield.

speaking in gasps mouths divest our secrets.
kissing you i swallow heat.

they study wealth in relation to denial.
construct lighting grids to eliminate all
shadows.

information drops off in
thin strands. in drift are viruses
identified as truth.

in standing waves obsidian fuses in clusters.
unnoticed. language is anaesthetized. cadence
cancelled. disturbance is managed.
prophets and rebels assassinated. non-believers
tortured on ultimate devices.

the dominants hide
receptors in trees after killing them. and in
walls of common buildings.
the rest obey,
plant seedlings in soil according to
televised instruction.

salt formations grow in caverns in every
throat. their heads convulse backward
and flap. they gasp for frequency
control. drown in dry close-up.

TO FORGET

pebbles of denial beneath his pain. under
the dura mater his chemicals have taken her
into his nuclei. pressed
against concrete he sweats, her
sweet milk wastes on his tongue. ghosts
                           exit
                                  his palms.

his teased taste for walnut
skin and lip
stick.

he paints as if he had frozen the light.
a cup rattles in his saucer as she writes.
he fills the cup to invent thought. she is
vivid outside him. he renames her history to
forget he has no sense of fashion.

empty blue pockets of night.

they weep.
          stars flash warnings.
across separate lakes.

light beams
in strata, bend
over the boulder field. no exit
breaks
        the skein.
polarizers diminish the wood, filter the
murmurous sea. high density
zones rumble incessantly.   dreams
atomize. residents touch with
monied hands. they speak in wartime codes whose
ciphers are forgotten. every
glance corners. every gaze
foreshortens. whitehot cylinders
deflect light, radiating heat
and lethal particles. hospitals own
the cemeteries. by night tropical
insects emerge
from body holes.

finger bones clatter on gun barrels. parades
celebrate soul's domestication, the wondrous
perfection of the power
grids.

A SPIRE

his mouth softens into hers   shudders her
belly   his chest tightens   bodies afire
in a press of skin

phantom walls throw open to the wind
the weightless ceiling of the dark
has no interior   no within
no consummation

they strain to stay outside a touch
hands ghost other walls,   rooms with lives
beyond the arch

one by one   brick on brick   a spire shapes (a
spirit place)   link to stones that
thrust, that stand, earth-
bound

at the shadow edge they
turn, barely touch   eyes yearn up and up
to see rock fly, flare
into smoke to veil them

nectar beads their lips

ash of regret dusts
their tongues

iii. tonguing

Soak the tongue overnight. If this is not possible, scrub it well, cover it with cold water, and bring it to the boil. Remove the tongue and discard the water. Rinse the tongue, return it to the kettle and cover it with boiling water. Bring to the boil, then simmer about four hours. Test with a fork to determine when done.

Standard recipe for tongue.

1.

a whisper
the book dead
a wish a
fishless hook
a vow with bowed heads
vespers prayer
vowels adrift soughing in narrow mouths
among consonants

all is naught
caught as we are
on barbs
by horizontal bars of negative
a plague of zeros
a zoo of dark cages, gates in wind
swinging open
& shut
pins in hinges squeal
pang for freed animals

we are penned
pacing on padded feet claws splintered
caught on the edge of a taper
on time's paperthin thinner sliver.
scared cities pinned to a crust
scanning an astonishment of stars cascading
through a scarcity of lenses

headstones are scoured
for words
in the wearing
down

for a trace
even in a faint
scar

2.

speak
burst forth against boredom, pundit & warrior
as a gory corker of a hot afternoon bears
down on the cerebellum

glory in the face of battle
the enemy swilling over
the hill's brow
fierce with electric scowls
a school of eels
scooped from sea floor
slithering into action
scouring the trenches
teething the army's heels

an easy kill.
fouls their might
mashes them to midden
& buries them in the midatlantic rift
where spiky worms, an urge of urchins, feed
seizing a feast

or to escape
follow the parchment map
lurch across parched sand
slice through ice fields
swim beneath rice paddies, the kernel of an idea floating
overhead, the sweetmeat of a lobe   earmarked
for burning lips   that mouth
approval and
reward

3.

when the cramps come pinching
nerves wince you to the ground
you fall, incapable of any wish
clenched in the muscled limb
clipwinged

but in all the flipping of your lids
the battering you take
   (the cake whose batter you would lick from a knife
   instead of this slicing pain)
sets pitch   outrages you
conflagrates the twigs & branches of your verve

   you explode
into torrid lava
spin ash that winters the horizon, verticality
disappearing at peaks
no peering penetrates
no gesticulation releases
the vertebrate shackle.
   the spasm induces collapse
beyond the aid of labile application to extremities
beyond any tablet's prophylaxis

4.

for example, pygopods – grebe and loon –
officially podicipedidae, gaviidae
not pipit nor horned lark
though they too are scant snippets of ornithology
whose wings flutter improvisatory riffs
a scattering of latin skipping through
an eschatology of species in danger
threat engendered by the presence of the upright, unsavoury poseur
disposer of everything
unmotivated but for profit and speed
smearing the dominion as if
in control at the debonair wheel
(wracked and pinioned)

there's a rat in the works
you might say
the anthropomorphism not wholly ironic
the smell is not mus decumanus
yet everyone jerks their feet from the floor
climbs on chairs
stares underneath abhorrent and squealing
distraught and distracted
but blind to the sniffsnouted sooth
the whiskered verity
clawfooted bonetailed truth:
it's the scrawny rodents huddling on chairs
·and birds have unfeathered the nests

this muddle is no jest
no prank of weather, a rankle in conditions
you can bank on a wrangle in the streets'
last days of traffic
a scramble to escape the bottleneck
by the bottlefed bottlechoked bogglebrained
wobblelegged foozling foiblers
who doddled&doodled too long when it mattered

5.

you gamble with words
roll the diecast impression
lollygag or leap into the plot
of a sentence
or a lesser duration
take a reprieve from grammatical behaviour

you loll in the moment
as it dissolves in the solvent of time
you go with the grain to avoid splinters
solve crosswords at a scroll-top desk
ski winter with a gallop
or dance gambado and plié
angle of ankles caught
in the net's perfect diamonds
a bend of knees lift of arms
skein or scapula
some boney mesh

a brush with fresh scones
baskets abundant with biscuits
imagined with lobster bisque, biting the tongue
the way the nostril tugs it
budraised to the feast

        let me phrase that again
        words nearly the same the logic more logical
        (less thrill then)

the oven door is open
the scent of the baking
never mind you get the idea
the words are redundant
overbaked as they say overdone
which is not the same as repetition
which does not   according to stein   exist
does not exist she said i say
though the jug is full of play
and serious too with a head
start intellectual jumpstart
and a bead of honey for sweetness

do the flowers talk
and are they heard above the buzzing

6. WORDS FOR ARISTOTLE

candlesticks fit in
a bottle
      drip
wax
flickers and glows
glitters on slick silverware
wicks pucker & pop the flame enlivened!
a mottle goboes on the walls
holding in loud music
of the lauding audience
their hands a fluttering upsurge, the air musky
dessert! dessert! let encores begin!

jab a finger in the fire
a digit in the metronome
baton the battuta through the melody
prod flameheart
cradle the thinshelled vulnerable egg
but coddle not the falsely precious stone

the bottle, green
effectively pale green
leaning toward amber
cast from grist in millions of particles
grit in the millet
that grates through life

let no gesture mock transcendence
we gather elements, but our eyes are not glass

our teeth are not skin
our palms are not enamel.
there in a hand the brass snuffer
or two fingers licked
that leave the trailing smoke, that puff, as
the stick and wheel bumps through the cloak and dagger game
leaves us haggard
broken rhymes and repetitions play
the hoax, while the real
joke pervades, infects our callow pores
with slogan carcinoma
our upturned faces festering with furans

prattle not
o flatulent gob
o apologetic mob
bodies and brains logotomized
our graces spent
we go where we lead ourselves with tallowy
will, shallow-chinned and bland-eyed
toddling or fullthrottle
into the valley of
the shadow

7.

excrescent the horned
one visible at distances
by its adornment.
adored and scoped buck
shot from a blind
by O blindminded boys
naming this a sport
a game of equals, skill
sure, some luck thrown in
but none for the fair game
                    the kill

suck gut : squint eye
stack deck : squeeze trigger
be one with prey :
shoulder gun's kick : pluck beast
from hill or grove drop it quick
free it from its fear   release its blood
before adrenalinefright
sours the meat

monadic thrill bond
goodsounding words are bound to the hunt
the clustering of men around a corpse
taste at the table a boon to the buds
a supplication to the stomach's complaints

O saviour, O predator
O collector of antler hatracks
bend low pray to

your prey's tongue, fluttering in your palm
press down your lips, kiss
its faltering heart, draw
stillwarm juice and sinew to kick-

                              start your virility
powder its horns testes hooves excrement, anything
for the sake of your
gonads impending diminuendo

8.

we are cast among stones bridge-arching hour-glassing
at once bold   & sceptical of thrust
tongue-strung we trust trepidation   talk gravity
bluster at beauty in the eye
at the sparkling tone of perception's sly
and wary flight. after all, anything
can happen.
a belt of asteroids
might pelt us. hold us up
leave us panting   pressed to land
on the boulder pavement, diving
earthward to the bereavement of flight

you have been warned
now shoulder the blast, be brave
be generous avoid the inward suck
of selfreflexivity
        fly
            out there
                accelerate to syntax speed
on wordward vector
syllablestorm is the weather to dress for

you cannot predict the vibrato
of reeds ridges rapideyemovement dreams
ripples siffles doodles on ebony keys
dark melodies that score the track   track the score
    a torrid sirocco leaves even
    the poised parched and arkless

starless nightfall   nightfull of pulsing light scatters
husks, unanswered riddles. so keep your eyes
keen. speak with alacrity clarity
shuck all you can
of the upcreeping dust

9.

the need to make sense
the need to lie
     either purity
the baseline ours
     to define
     to defile

the speaker's integrity ingenuity
     mouth played against brain
shifts the point of reference, a seed
cast thisway or that
upwind downdale

you step for
protection to the bottom
of a swale, you lose
the horizon (words at a distance)

what of wit in the mix?

you can farm out your brain your body
no harm will come to it they say   give it to us
we'll make you rich
or thin
you can win
can have more or less, whichever
comes first, we'll make you
someone else then
all will be well

hell speaking of purity none of us
has it, we all walk as lies
all right i'll admit some of us are
driven by sensation some angst
some anachronous wish for sincerity
simplicity, for oldfashioned honesty
but notice the mould growing there from neglect
in these circumspect circum
locutionist times. logofaced clocks
won't show us the hour and what can we hear
through infozapped ears or see
pixeleyesed?

time to get with the zeitgeist
zero in it's all in the mouth
read my lips prime your tongue
get used to the taste of distaste

10. VESSEL
after fred wah & bpNichol

apple in air
calling your name
through some other acuity
pull neither here
nor in opposite directions
the inner tug appeals
lineal, innate
overcoming inertia
its lightheaded allure
of the moon's green
promise, bitten or
cupped in tongue, a curl
suspended
fruit of the unblinded
window

iv. spurious spurs : deft initions

The poet is a counter-punching radio.
— Jack Spicer

a.

Members of the aristarchy
we don't need your attitude. You are too
arch. Show no love for your subjects. You
prefer hollow airs and severity. You
follow us. Admit it. You sniff
at our boots. At our wrists.
No risk in your venture. No regard.
We won't mention your name in our works.
Though the tension that lurks where you probe
results in a thick critiphobia.

b.

Lay the banket by the foundation. I'll fill it
with wet clay or a fired rod when I detect
the procedure.
I'll cover or leave it bare
to air. Who will tell me?
I recognise some of the tools. And to a point
I'm versed on the principles.
But there's rank to contend with. Unclarified rules.
And the scaffold grows higher.
Such is the plight of the hod-carrier.

c.

You might call him swell. You might call him cur.
Or harmless curriedow. Just for show.
A test for you? Test for him? Most likely
both. How to know?
Little redemption is found in his smile once
it's seen through. Flattery gets him a mile.
Gets him around. Hurry now, be certain of yourself
be safe from his seasoned grin. Be clear. Know
his reason. Best for you? Better for him? Count
on the latter.

d.

for Anne Szumigalski

For some, joy. For some, despond.
For all an unknowing bound. What can you know?
What can be dreamed?
What can a sage see of the future
that never comes? Never can come.
You depend on faith. Questions are out,
no question.
You've come out of your shell
with clammy hands to attend your desponsage.
You are a sponge for chance. Ready to dance
to the shimmy tune or the plaintive blues. Ready
to two-step to the band.

e.

Out of hand. Or in hand. A relay. A delay.
A reality of bearing or befitting. Buffeted
by terrain or temporary setbacks.
Some have been shot upon arrival. Successors learn to beware.
To expediate the task as asked. If wise, with speed. Then
scarcity. Relate words of warning to their kind
Carrying Carrying out Carrying on   They are best
prepared
by preparation.

f.

In one swell foupe. Poof. Pop. All at once. Effort-
less. A hawk to the coop. Sweeping dip. Slip through air.
A clock through the swoop of the day. Imperceptible soupstop
on the day's magnificent arc. The card of the hour
disappearing.   Sleight hand. Swirl
of silk. Transcendence.
Feather flourish. Zenith. Nadir. Zen
ith.

g.

Don't get me gosting. I can be a bear. Unbearable.
I'm not boasting. No sense pretending.
I foster low threshold for nonsense.
Hot temper. Foul disposition. They come naturally.

I raise hackles. Like a weed in the grass. I'm
maligned. Despised.
Searched out by the scythe's bare blade. It
can't cut me off its effects. Yet
the cleaver's existence puts me on
edge. Makes me growl.

h.

Herald. His uniformity. Well-informed
by proximity to certain information, borne in his pouch.
He's proxy for the sender.
No slouch in delivery, no
matter what degree the news bodes. Heels click.
Conform. Digits peak. About face.
No taste for frontline heroics. Or casual casualty.
His cause: communication harboured to extremes. From
here to there. There to here. Bold link.
The herebode. Furtive
slinker. Between the poles.

i.

A Matter of Ego?

A Matter of Selection.

Bricks over Bread.
Coca-Cola over Water.
Getting over Giving.
Instamatic over Meditation.
Killing over Kindness.
Listing over Making.
Motoring over Strolling.
Stealth Jets over Innu.
Watching over Seeing.

Done over, over-
done.

A deadly exchange.

No wonder.

For a change. For an innuent change. Choose
the intrinsic act.

j.

By jowls the current howls
if you hear it in the cells. Dry, wet, etcetera.
Don't expect to put a face to it.
Bones for poles.
The septum bridge. The quantum leap in electrolyte.
Sleek and headfirst. Head and heel.
You are attracted to your opposite. And vice versa.
In reaction the tissues charge. By joves the power flows.

k.

He has the way. A sensitivity, intuitive. Yes
he sniffed it out. Followed his protuberance, so to speak.
Where others saw a mound he sensed a kernel, a seed
that sprouted the whole field of vision. He
kerned the situation; unmasked the facts and
caught the fallout. Defused, dismantled, dismissed with his three-
fold skill. Triple agent. Double diplomacy. All dealt
with modesty. Even kindness. No doubt.
According to him, it's not learned.
Birth is the key.

1.

Silence is in arrears, or so it appears, behind
on payments to the usurers. The dons are in cahoots,
absconding with tranquillity. They play treble and bass
on cash registers, something terrible. And everything in between. Nothing
but trouble, and otherwise thunderous rumble.
Leave the world loudful. Full of fullness. Empty
of   . Outside and inside my head. Collisions
of comets and organs. Seems like forever.
Can't think myself out of here. Or somewhere else. No
sonic solution. No tonic relief. Face it, the collusion's embedded.
I'm bereft.

m.

Improper use of musculature. Of cavity. Embouchure.
And air. No instrumentalist.
We're talking talk.
Not a talker. Certainly not an elocutionist.
More chatter than chat.
You never heard such momblishness. Never will.
Into his chin. His hat. His tea or beer. No ear can fathom
the syllables missed. Can't hear what can't be heard.
Turn away. Find something to attend.
Something that meets you halfway. That uses its capacities.
You'll find yourself speaking up.
Overexerting the lips and tongue.

n.

Beachless beachball. Bouffant in a shower.
Bustles without thrust. Collapsed lung. Concave mirrors.
Condom the next morning.
Egoless ego. Gimpy pillows. Hackneyed haiku.
Leaky balloons, their wrinkles. Cock in cold.
Non-plouffed soufflé.
Pooling ice cream. Kwinzee in May.
Raisins. Sliver moon. Shattered heart.
Slumped cake. Unrewarding popcorn.
Next morning, unused condom.
Unexpected endings.

o. *

Only the hand in circles. A slow and steady round. Effort.
Discerning application of the self.
The nearly perfect touch. Just so. And back and forth.
Piece by piece. Spot by spot. Leading to the whole.
Body leaning in. Ounding the fleece. Till every whisker
gleams. Skin of persimmon. Grackle neck. Suede
gloves well-used. Woman with gracious bearing. Windglazed
snowdrift. Man of humble demeanour. Down of thistle.
Sheen abounding.
O!

p.

Pardon me.
I'll tell you in a minute.
But first.
Or I don't know how to put it.
Familiar phrases.
Like a river's course. Or appearance of holes
in Swiss cheese. Not to be confused with any kind of board
game. Or Italian sauce. Yet
spurring you on. And hunger. What purpose is served?
Perhaps an underscore. A parataxis.
Perhaps, like a river, it resolves its obstacles.
I'm not optimistic.
Sponge. Fueller of frustration. No pride in parechesis.
Simply avoidance.
Pummelling the shrubbery.
Most often the hour's usurper.

q.

Query antiquity. Quantify the mysteries. Take your cue.
The quest: to say it all in alphabets.
Magic speaks unlettered from earth's crust. Grit.
Granite. Grain of sandstone. Quill. Eloquent

Tongue. Probe the quadrune for ancestral evidence.
Poke beneath quitch. In the quarries. Or deeper.
Sometimes the mantle helps. Quakes to reveal. Temper.
Texture. Yields and repeals artifacts.

We too often obey the line. Question the evident.
Fear dustborne quinsy that causes catarrh. Persistent cough.
Repetitive swallows. Loons. Quetzal. Birds arrive.
Ahead of us to sing of things we cannot sense. Quintessence.

We need to qualify. To square off meaning.
Need to underscore. Understand. Beneath the quotidian.
Would the quixotic (can you know
who you are?) please step forward. Quickly now. Jump the
queue.

r.

Rope frays with the sway of the sunken boat. Season whose line is
missed dismisses poets. Sails full of unreasonable Hope.
Despair. Or Rage. Rage against the Dying of. Why bother? Most
are wayward, not well-versed. Oh, the usual Lament. No care. No
regard. Empirical rhymers. Lyrical whiners. But wait. Poets
are wordweighed. Their souls ribaudred. And
Pure. Reminded by a bullet in the wrist. The risk of
hallucination. Hammeredhead reality. All that matters may be
meter in the end. I am pent up. Pulsed and rippled skin rising
in bumps. Pores ascending to meet the clamber. The climber
turns it all on cord. To song. Voice. Vestige. The vessel
tilts. Reaches new heights before the slip. Unbridled. Tidal.
Symbiotic. Styx. Ur. Sombre. Whirr. Swirl. Splinter.

.

s.

Slicing bite. Twinned incisors. Keen.
Knife or. Introducing to the unified, separation.
Making of one, two. Or none.
Or of the separate – of two (intimate) – one. One
never knows. Gesture: lunge, swipe, open & close
thumb & finger. In each an opening.
This scising paradox.
Grate or glide of edges. Turns
things inside
out. Death always
lingers,

t.

Tremble. Tumble.
Nothing to do with tongue. Or does it? Palate. Roll.
Telluric. Resolve. Ocean motion. The best machine.
Or metal drum with pumice. Smoothes jagged
corners. Roundness resounds. All symmetry.
Surface. Ecstasis. Explosion.
Transmitting
outward. Mellifluent to touch.

To induce delirium. Take in
lust Dry or wet Stir Polish Orb it Tumulate
Tingle Lustre Fondle Orbit

u.

Up.   Up.
Comes   pneuma.
Upsurge.   Ultimate
release. Uvula   riff. Tongue
pulse.   Teeth.   Lips.   Beneath   sense   the   pendulum.

Period.   Swung.
Amplitude.   Symmetry.
Arc mirrored.   Mirrored arc.
Ascending. Glide.   Ride up. Slide.
Imperceptibly. Gasp.   Gusto slips inevitably.
Gust of fussy wind   pushes us   just short of destinations.

Takes   breath.
Smuggler.   Deceiver.
Under cover.   Operation.
Illicit ululation.   Ulwhurft. Cough.
Out. Expire. Released to rest. Curve emptied.   Cavity.   No
time.   No valiant cavalier defends.   No cavil.   No caveat.
No emperor. No entrepreneur.   No particle physicist.   No
solution. Absolute.   Ruffle.   Flutter.   Puff.   Untimely.

Impromptu.

v. *

Vanity. Fish scales. Rust.

Such call forth the vasker. Grease of elbow. Gleam is next to
You-know-who-liness.

A nice device. For shaving. (Lather up). Ice. Stubble of
face, legs, underarms, flaking paint.

Each scrape reveals the virginal. Husking vetch. Maple wood
bevelled on the lathe. Skin abraded on gravel. Enamel cave
beneath decay in carries. Gouging the vug.
Valley dug by retreating glacier. Bone cleaning beetles. A
velvet comb. Scourer of salt-encrusted vessels. For each job
there is a proper tool.

Volute carver. Each stroke a new invention.

w.

What we must protect. Preserve. Best to walk with waders.
Squish. Squish. Fowl alight if essence is not fouled.

Grass in spring deluge. Gurgling where you place your feet.
Fun if shoeless. Squish. Squish. Such pleasure is way-laid
for dignity. Maturity. So stiff. Proper. Not the wild way.
Too much might spur vertigo. Spontaneity.

Fear the weir. Rising level upstream. Terrible downside
undertow. Guard against the revel.

Constant inhalation hoards against a deficit. Holding causes
quease. The panic stroke. Without deep breath. Improper
pranayama. Embracing nada to deny nadam.

No time to waste! Rush! Seek reeds! Hail cattails! Swish
through lily pads! Greens in hydroponic gardens. Tune in
water music. Hydrophonic marsh cacophony. Leap into a soggy
bog! Wade. Waist deep if necessary. Squish! Squish! In the
weasy wash. Wallow!

x.

Extemporize. Whatever can be mobilized.

Box twirling on its corner. Plates spinning on sticks. A hex
spun out of pointed phrases. What taxes make you do. Repeated
tonguetrilled sax riff. Round and round, the waxing rag in
hand. The whirring brush in xesturgy. Flux of day dependent
on the mix. Spin.

Hospitality expressed with a whirl of generosity. Gestures.
The host in xyque amidst the strangers. Xenial rapport exudes
enthusiasm. Fascination. Assured. And experienced. Dizziness
disguised. Short and tall tales unfurl the words. Flourish.
Shift axis.

Exhilarate. Keep feet in the reel. Hands on the wheel. Eyes
on the gyration. Motion is perpetual if laxity can't set in,
if there's no fix. No kinks in the works. No jinx.

y.

Yerked. The lock tumbles. Groan of ancient stocks. Close
easier than open. Easier to accommodate weight. Mistook as
wings. The zygomatic dilemma. Binary. Binding. Blind.
Boneyoked. Cellbound. Soulswiped.

You can yank when you think you feel it. But it hardly moves.
Clamps the neck. Stills the groin. Sometimes we get
panicky. Even yell. Yowl. Flash our eyes in desperation. Snap
Yashica, Sony for the archive.

We give up yes for no. Accommodate the heaviness
voluntarily. Spirit yields to shackle. Will not fly. No
will. Restrained so. Search too late for the visionary. The
way. Out. Bound by the yiyet. Compliant. Helpless. Why

z. *

Zest loses all track of this. No matter the zone. Each
margin sets tempo between. Zeugma's compression saves space
but confuses. Becomes a puzzle. Pieces do not fit. Sense of
synchronicity subsumed in a quiz. Tick. Tick. Tick. Muddle in
the mental maze. Gazing through gauze.

Dedication is required. Attention to the brew with
timing. Zymurgy. Ingredients and art. Or in cooking.
Precision yields perfect zwieback.

Zucchini is seasonal. Seems to happen overnight. Relies on
proper sequence. Leaf. Flower. Buzz. And always water,
sunlight. You must know when to pluck it. A sense of
occasion. Such as, a priest doffing his zucchetto.

Tick. Tick. Tick. When dancing be the beat. Fit the
zeitgeist. In swirling zimme ignore the dizziness. Sizzle!
Don't doze! Feel zeal!

v. a game to be played

dedicated to Bob Cobbing

TESTED & PROVED

rapid reading brings rapid rewards
full sense of, the easy-
to-follow words cut
ting time

why do you read so slowly?

no need to stamp!

everything that is written
increases the pleasure
pleasure snatched
– a remarkable degree –
in precious leisure

NOBODY WAVED

twisting together
the wheels of industry
lie
heavy on
pursuit of pleasure

intertwining parts
remove sense
shackle
dull &
plastic man
– what he wishes to do, desires –
with rope

customers come
to close
quarters
watch unconcerned
indulge their own
silence
        d
            dreams

soldiers have rarely won wars
they fear snakes
hear voices
hallucinate positive & negative stimuli
flourish in confused & dangerous times

prisoners' selfsearchings
symbolize the reversal
merely entertaining
a variety of chambers

contemplating
the social atom
both wind up
repeatedly falling

study at leisure
shows you the way
through the medium
showing you how
for pleasure
boring rail sea & airplane trips
keep on selling

ambition can't lose
all you supply
will be refunded
if you have not
recovered

UMBRA

the dark region of a shadow
    usually elliptical
lies
        (no weight)
inside an object

absorbed by the homogeneous medium
the time required
(an imaginary straight line
falling vertically)
has superseded visual observation

the appearance of a dark ligament
has blasted away the outer layers
ejected
their mutual attraction

A GAME TO BE PLAYED

your reflection
like a criminal
  at times terrifying
thrived on secrecy

you shrunk to bare essentials
adjusted to reveal
inherent dramas, gripping
a reputation for
unflattering traumas

plunged to an unexplored region
only attempts at pornographic
immortality
transformed
for the worse
the quality
of being
alive

VIRTUAL INDIVIDUALITY

celibacy is fashionable
perhaps you're one
now giving it serious thought

& suddenly you feel
an air of desire
what you want
may be out of reach
something sensitive, reassuring
romantic opium

with conscientious use
coming
has certain advantages

there's no time
like the present

the gentleman with the shotgun
had fears
altered states
existential frustration
greed for pleasure

clouded by drama
footsteps in the dark
escalate the stimulation

sensory pleasure
eventually palls

nuns flashy ladies fluff tarts
you have to be loaded
hot & indolent
fire & water

tempted?
fancy a weep?
come
blow away your troubles
off the front foot
turn tummy bulge
(which great & strong men find
irresistible) zip away the enemy within
moving eye
brows to twitch

the national union
& sponsored coalition enterprise board
was to leave
the company file shut
on slump solidarity

recently
ways to combat people
by the nation
have indeed
been in

we fit &
merely other defendants
of the low lying areas
launch rivers in devon
twice a week
for improved specification
in the fall of industrial action

only when they feel immoral
men & women
half want
a healthy development

nobody in the twentieth century
keeps it long enough

by full methods of persuasion
they willingly
   consciously or unconsciously
strangle it at birth

PATH

alibis shift history
block ability to know
form rifts that touch
man & woman who
stumbling
look cautiously for symbols
a path too
difficult to hold

words turn back in mouths
you who want product
& watching
spill blood
on only distant hands

victory consists of amounts
worn down or built unjustly
is kind as milk
in split stomachs

loss is constant truth
this duality
back
& forth
this twisting
                    fall

NOTHING MUCH HAPPENS

jaded with itself
razzmatazz
remote control
on the nations' tv screens
has not demurred
attending to
ritual functions

AFTERWORD

This book is dedicated to bpNichol (1944-1988), friend and mentor, who read early drafts of poems in *a stranger's dream* and encouraged me to continue. I am eternally grateful for the encouragement and friendship he gave me over 15 years.

Bob Cobbing, dedicatee of the section *a game to be played* is the British sound and concrete poet whose cut-up poems inspired me to take up the game.

The section *spurious spurs: deft initions* uses, as catalysts to individual poems, words selected from The Compact Edition of the Oxford English Dictionary's (1971) *List of Spurious Words* "(arising chiefly from misprints or misreadings) that have been current in English dictionaries or other books of some authority". In this *List*, spurious words appear with their definitions. To generate his poems the author selected one word from each alphabetic section. Where there was a word listed under a particular alphabetic character, but no definition, the author invented his own definition as a starting point; where there was no word at all, the author invented his own spurious word and its definition, then proceeded with the compositional concept. The spurious word is included in its resulting poem. In this section, the pieces *d, o, v, z,* are dedicated to Anne Szumigalski, as indicated by the asterisk *.

I want to thank Dennis Cooley for accepting some of these pieces to include among the first chapbook publications of Pachyderm Press in 1993. And my gratitude has doubled in 1998, for Cooley's close read, understanding, and suggestions, in the final editing of this entire manuscript. Some poems in this work have benefited from critical readings by Barbara Klar, Gerry Shikatani, John L. Clark, Susan Andrews Grace and Elizabeth Philips.

I wish to acknowledge several organizations who have supported this writing. For financial aid I thank the Individual Assistance Programs of the Saskatchewan Arts Board and the Canada Council, and the Writers Reserve Program of the Ontario Arts Council. Thanks too to the Saskatchewan Writers Guild's invaluable Writers' & Artists' Colonies which provided retreats where I worked on the manuscript.

ACKNOWLEDGEMENTS

Some of these poems have previously appeared in: *white cycle* (*KON-TAKTE* Series 1, Volume 4, 1977); *a game to be played* (Writers Forum, 1981); *What #3*, 1985; *dwarf puppets on parade*, issue #1, 1987; *Cross Canada Writer's Quarterly*, V. 9 # 3/4, 1987; *The Swift Current Anthology* (Coach House Press, 1987); *fluttertongue* (chapbook, Pachyderm Press, 1993); *Where the Voice Is Coming From*, Vol. II, 1994*)*; and *Prairie Fire*, V.15, #2 (1994), V. 16, #2 (1995), and V. 18, #1 (1997).

PERMISSIONS

Printed in September 1998 by

ON DEMAND PRINTING INC.

in Boucherville, Quebec